D1367135

STRANGE STORIES OF LIFE

by
Joann A. Lawless

A

cpi

Book

From

RAINTREE PUBLISHERS
Milwaukee

11 12 13 14 15 16 17 18 19   95 94 93 92 91 90

Library of Congress Number: 77-10760

Art and Photo Credits

Cover illustration by Lynn Sweat
Photo on page 9, Jen and Des Bartlett/Bruce Coleman, Inc.
Illustrations on pages 11, 15, 18, 24, 29, 32, 34, 38, 40, 42, 44, 46 and 48, Jeffrey Gatrall.
Photo on page 16, Wide World Photos, Inc.
Photo on page 22, Len Rue, Jr./Bruce Coleman, Inc.
Photo on page 37, the Granger Collection, New York.
All photo research for this book was provided by Sherry Olan.
Every effort has been made to trace the ownership of all copyrighted material in this book and to obtain permission for its use.

Library of Congress Cataloging in Publication Data

Lawless, Joann A. 1949-
    Strange stories of life.

    SUMMARY: Curious tales, supposedly true, of people, animals, and natural phenomena.
    1. Curiosities and wonders—Juvenile literature. [1. Ckuriosities and wonders] I. Title.
AG243.L36   001.9′3   77-10866

Manufactured in the United States of America.
ISBN 0-8172-1062-8 lib. bdg.
ISBN 0-8172-2167-0 softcover

Contents

Chapter 1
Some Amazing Animals   5

Chapter 2
The Astounding Plants   21

Chapter 3
Watch Out for Nature's Tricks   27

Chapter 4
Puzzling People   41

As far as can be told, the stories in this book are true. They are the amazing stories of unusual animals, plants, and people. Each story is a challenge—to what you have learned about living creatures and to your imagination.

Chapter

1

SOME AMAZING ANIMALS

The Dog Who Wanted to Go Home

One day at a gas station in Indiana, a man and his small dog, Bobbie, waited for their car to be fixed. Suddenly, a pack of wild dogs chased Bobbie away from his owner's car. A few yards from the gas station Bobbie began to fight with a ferocious bull terrier. Smaller than the dog he was fighting, Bobbie turned and ran as fast as he could. He continued until he had run quite far from the station.

Poor Bobbie ran around in circles and made several false starts trying to find his owner. What he didn't realize was that he and his owner had been on vacation in Indiana. They were heading for home—*in Oregon*. Unable to find Bobbie for hours, the saddened owner had gotten into his car to make the long journey—alone.

But Bobbie was going to go home. Although lost in Indiana, the dog began a trip that would finally take him over 3,000 miles. The dog crossed icy rivers, hot deserts, mountains, rocky plains, and farmlands. He even swam the Mississippi River. Sometimes people along the way would help him when he needed food and shelter. But Bobbie never stayed in one place very long. This horrible and exhausting journey took six months.

Bobbie's owner had given up all hope of ever seeing his dog again. Imagine his surprise when, one morning, he looked out his front window to see a limping dog coming up the walk.

With bloodied paws, swollen legs, three missing teeth, and lots of scars, Bobbie had come home. His owner was shocked. How had Bobbie found his way?

Bobbie's owner set out to trace the dog's incredible journey. Along the way he found the many people who had helped Bobbie. No one could believe that Bobbie had made the amazing journey. But Bobbie and his owner believed it. *Bobbie was home.*

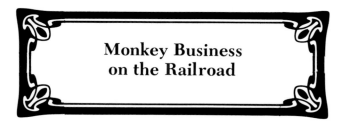

Monkey Business on the Railroad

James Wide had lost both of his legs in an accident while working on an African railroad in 1877. After his accident, Wide got a new job as a signalman. He could operate the track switching and handle his other duties on this job while sitting in a wheelchair. Some friends found Wide a little shack by the railroad so he could be close to his work. When he wasn't working, Wide spent most of his time with his pet baboon named Jack and tending his garden. No one could really say that Wide spent any of his time caring for the baboon. It seemed just the opposite—*Jack took care of his owner.*

Jack the baboon pumped and hauled water from the well. He cleaned the shack and he weeded the garden. Every morning, after breakfast, the baboon locked the house and pushed Wide to work in his wheelchair. This was done in a very special way. Wide had a special wheelchair built to run on rails. But caring for his handicapped owner was only a small part of the baboon's daily routine. *Jack also helped to run the railroad.*

Amazingly, over several months the baboon learned to work the levers that set the signals for the railroad. He was soon operating all the controls that opened and closed the track switches. Jack seemed to know the train schedule and the exact time, each day, when tracks had to be switched.

In nine years on the job, Jack the baboon *never* made a mistake nor did he cause so much

Although he had never been hired, Jack helped run the railroad. Jack was a Kenyan baboon, as is the thoughtful-looking fellow pictured here.

9

as a near-accident. And in the nine years he as-
sisted the signalman, the baboon never missed
a day's work. Jack, an African baboon, became
the first animal ever to run a railroad!

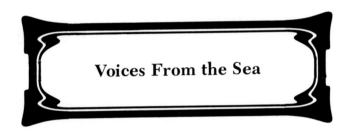

Voices From the Sea

If the baboon is intelligent, then the dolphin
must be considered a *genius*! In fact, the dolphin's brain has been found to work 16 times
faster than the human brain. Dolphins can learn to
turn a switch (like the one Jack operated for the
railroad) in one lesson. Baboons need over a
hundred. But the really unbelievable thing
about dolphins is that they seem able to *talk*
with each other.

Dolphins seem to make two kinds of sounds.
One is very much like a human whistle. The
other is a series of rapidly repeated *clicks*. There
have been many scientific studies of the amazing

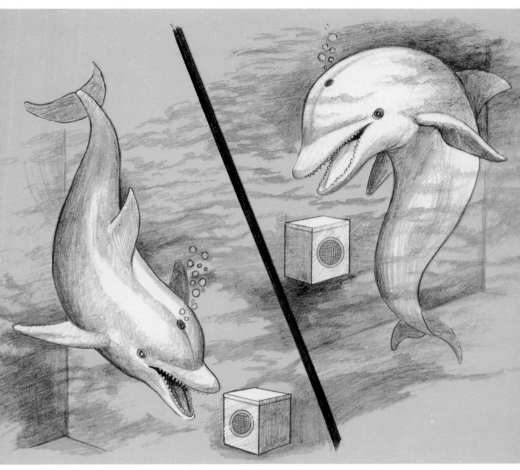

Dolphins are close to humans in their ability to observe, to learn, and to solve problems. As an example, two dolphins were observed chasing an eel. The eel slipped into a hole. One dolphin grabbed a small poisonous stinging fish and stuffed it into the hole. The eel jumped from its hiding place and the chase continued.

dolphins. In one experiment, two dolphins were reported to have talked over a telephone in a pool at the U. S. Naval Ordinance Testing Station in Pasadena, California.

11

Doris and Dash, a dolphin couple, were placed in two separate soundproof tanks in a pool. Each tank had an underwater telephone that could send and receive voice messages. Scientists could stop conversation over the telephones whenever they liked. But Doris and Dash outsmarted the scientists. The dolphins appeared to know instantly when their connection had been broken.

Doris and Dash would speak briefly for about five seconds—each time. Then each would stop and wait for an answering sound. When one didn't get an answer from the other, the dolphin would stop talking. An even more remarkable thing happened. The dolphins seemed to stop talking if they thought the scientists were listening in on their conversations!

The dolphin voice is five times higher in pitch than a human's, and the dolphin language can carry ten times as much information as a human message. Doris and Dash were faster and better talkers than the scientists studying them. But there *is* another difference between the dolphin phone calls and the ones we make. *Dolphins never have to pay a high telephone bill!*

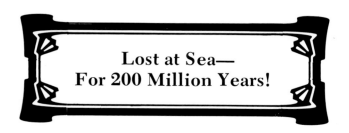

Lost at Sea—
For 200 Million Years!

Another amazing sea creature is—or *was*—the *coelacanth* (SEEL-a-kanth). The creature lived 200 million years ago, even before the dinosaur. With its short stumps—now thought to be the beginnings of legs—it could swim or walk along the ocean floor. The coelacanth was believed to be the first sea creature to leave the water and spend time on the land.

The earliest known coelacanth fossil is over 70 million years old. Scientists were sure the animal had long since vanished from the earth. Then, less than 50 years ago, scientists had some second thoughts. A fisherman startled the world!

In December, 1938, the captain of a fishing boat hooked a strange fish about 250 feet below the surface of the Indian Ocean. The fish, steel blue with very large scales, was about 5 feet long and weighed 125 pounds.

The captain hauled it in and took it to the Albany Museum in Grahams, South Africa. The scientists at the museum were amazed and no wonder. The fish looked like a coelacanth. But it was alive! How could a prehistoric fish still be alive? Were there others still swimming the sea? The fish died a few days later, before Professor J. L. B. Smith at the museum could prove whether it was a coelacanth.

South African scientists sent hundreds of letters to fishermen all over the world. They offered a reward to anyone who could capture a coelacanth. It took 14 years, but they finally got an answer.

In 1952 an old fisherman pulled in a huge, strange-looking fish about 200 miles off the shores of the Comoro Islands, a group of French islands between Madagascar and the coast of eastern Africa. Because he had never seen this type of fish, he showed it to a friend. The friend remembered the scientist's letter years before and contacted the South African museum. Had another ancient sea giant been discovered?

Professor Smith flew in on a special government plane. He examined the fish and cried, "*It*

Reward   Offered

COELACANTH

How could the five to six foot long prehistoric fish have been pulled from the water in 1938? Would there ever be another one found?

is another coelacanth!" The "return of the coelacanth" was hailed as one of the most astounding biological discoveries of the century.

Scientists are still trying to figure out how the fish survived. And now they may have another modern wonder to ponder. As recently as July, 1977, a Japanese fishing boat brought in a portion of a recently killed sea creature. Al-

The decomposed body of a strange, prehistoric sea animal that was brought up by a Japanese fishing boat. Perhaps it was a plesiosaur—a prehistoric marine reptile with a small head, long neck, four paddle-like limbs, and a short tail. The plesiosaur is a prime suspect for the role of *Loch Ness Monster*.

though the fishing boat captain threw the fish body back, pictures were taken first. Scientists think the fish was a *plesiosaur*, a sea animal that was supposed to have completely died off a million years ago.

A fish, long thought dead, returns to haunt scientists. Quite a story, but suppose the same creature you thought you had just killed came back and *bit* you? Professor Fred Medem, a Smithsonian scientist, was bitten twice in a Brazilian lagoon by a reptile called a *caiman*, whose neck he had broken. The caiman is smaller than the crocodile or alligator. "Somehow," said the scientist, "the caiman's jaw can react independently of the rest of its nervous system. Even dead, the jaw can move. And it's [bite is] quite painful."

The Largest Spider

A spider as large as a gorilla? *Impossible?* Scientists tell us it is not only possible, but it was actually so. Giant spiders roamed this earth 300

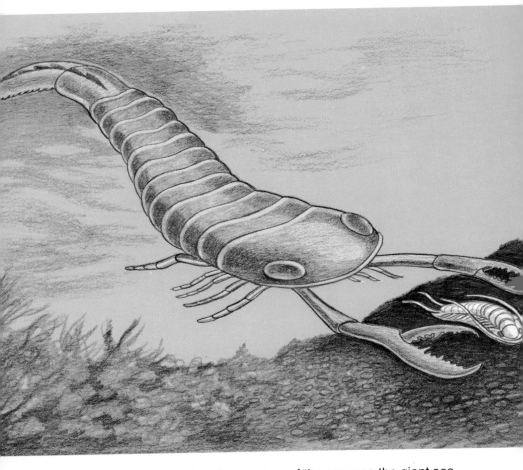

One of the prehistoric monsters of the sea was the giant sea scorpion—a creature dangerous at both ends of its body. To the rear was a poisonous stinger while up front it had huge, grasping claws.

million years ago. When the world was covered with warm, quiet seas, giant sea scorpions swam with their huge, free-swinging claws. These spiders measured up to nine feet long!

18

And Speaking of Animals . . .

. . . the all-time biggest animal in the world is a mammal—the *blue whale.* The largest blue whale ever caught was in 1912 in Argentina—over 110 feet long and almost 200 tons, equal to the combined weight of over 30 African elephants!

. . . the smallest fish in the sea is the *Marshall Islands goby*—less than half an inch long, weighing 2 milligrams. To bring in a 1 ounce catch, a fisherman would need almost 18,000 of these fish!

. . . the speediest creature in the world is a bird—*the spine-tailed swift.* The bird can fly at speeds of more than 105 miles per hour!

Before you read the next chapter, here is a riddle to answer:

They are big—the tallest giants ever on earth.

They are strong—stronger than elephants or army tanks.

They are very old—some are more than 4,000 years old—yet they are still alive and growing.

What are these modern-age monsters that live everywhere in the world?

Chapter

2

THE ASTOUNDING PLANTS

The oldest, strongest, tallest living things still growing on earth are trees. The giant sequoias in California grow to 300 feet or more. Some of them are 1,000 years old! The *bristlecone* pine (*Pinus arista*) has been growing for 4,800 years, even before Moses is said to have received the Ten Commandments. These pines, called "living driftwood," live in the *Methuselah Grove* in California. (Methuselah, a Biblical man, was said to have lived for 969 years.)

This bristlecone pine of California has been growing for 4,600
years. There are no older trees known on earth. In March, 1974
this tree was reported to have produced almost 50 live seedlings.

The bristlecone pines still produce seeds from which new trees grow. These trees survive at elevations up to 11,000 feet. The looks of bristlecone pine trees have been changed over time by the effects of wind, fire, and ice. Incredibly, some of them can be seen growing almost parallel to the ground with most of their roots exposed. The bristlecone pine grows just one inch every 100 years.

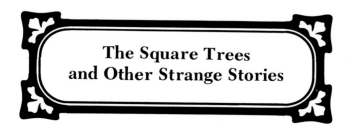

The Square Trees and Other Strange Stories

A few miles north of the Panama Canal Zone is the "Valley of the Square Trees." It is the only place in the world where trees have perfectly square trunks. The trees are *cottonwoods*, and they are a great unexplained mystery to scientists. No one knows why the trunks and the age rings grow square in shape.

Farther south, in Venezuela, there is the *planta del mudo*. It looks like sugar cane, but

The *planta del mudo* stem looks much like sugar cane, but no one who knows the plant would treat it like sugar cane!

don't try eating the stems. You will lose your voice for up to 48 hours. This plant is so strange —*it will leave you speechless.*

In Sierra Madre, California, grows an amazing *Chinese wisteria*. This Chinese wisteria looks like a vast field filled with delicate flowers. Yet what looks like a whole field of flowers is just one plant!

Planted in 1892, this single plant covers an entire acre and has branches over 500 feet long. Unbelievably, this plant weighs more than 252 tons. For 5 weeks each year, the Chinese wisteria has 1½ million blossoms.

The largest rose tree known is called the *Lady Banksia*. It is 9 feet high and covers over 5,380 square feet. This tree is supported by 68 posts and 1,000 feet of piping. The Lady Banksia stands near the Rose Tree Inn Museum in Tombstone, Arizona. *Its blossoms could fill the ballroom of a palace.*

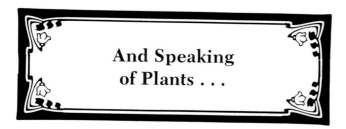

And Speaking of Plants . . .

. . . the biggest living thing in the world is the *General Sherman*—a tree in the Sequoia National Park in California. The *General Sherman* isn't the tallest tree (it's only 272.3 feet high), but its trunk is more than 79 feet around. The weight of the *General Sherman* is figured to be about 2,150 tons!

. . . another California tree—the *Howard Libbey Tree* in Redwood Creek Grove—stands over 365 feet tall, making it the tallest tree in the world!

. . . if people say you are "growing as fast as a weed," tell them about the *Eucalyptus* trees on the Pacific island of New Guinea. One of these trees has grown 35 feet in just 15 months. It is the fastest growing tree in the world!

. . . and if you want a fast growing weed to tell them about, try the *giant kelp*—a Pacific Ocean seaweed. It can grow almost 18 inches in a single day, and a single plant can reach lengths of close to 200 feet!

Chapter

3

WATCH OUT
FOR
NATURE'S TRICKS

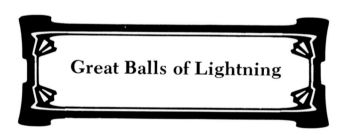

Great Balls of Lightning

On November 29, 1969, an Eastern Airlines night flight between New York City and Washington, D.C., flew through a bad electrical storm. A passenger in one of the front seats was looking out the window. From the corner of his eye he saw something strange behind him. He turned to find a bolt of lightning *inside the plane* —moving down the aisle and heading straight for him. It traveled, straight as a bullet, down the center of the aisle. As quickly as it appeared, the bolt vanished.

Mr. and Mrs. Robert B. Greenlee, a couple living in Dunnellon, Florida, sat on their patio with a next-door neighbor. One of the women was swatting some annoying flies. There was a slight drizzle and the sound of thunder in the distance.

One large fly was particularly annoying. It buzzed from place to place, but it never seemed to land. Then it came to rest on the table. Just as the woman swatted at the fly, a ball of white light appeared three feet in front of her. It seemed to have a fuzzy glow around its edges. The startled woman dropped her fly swatter. And at that same moment, she heard an explosion that sounded like a blast from a shotgun. The flash was a ball of lightning.

The *ball* hit the patio pavement. Then suddenly it vanished. No one on the patio was hurt, but a nearby neighbor's electric stove shorted out at about the same time. Another neighbor 50

For a while all that disturbed this Dunnellon, Florida family were some buzzing flies. What followed the flies made the evening unforgettable!

feet away also heard the blast. She remarked to the woman, "You sure got *that* fly!"

The lightning on the plane and the Florida patio are just two examples of a strange phenomenon called *ball lightning*. Sometimes the *lightning balls* are the size of peas. Other times they might be the size of a house. Their flash can appear in violet, red, yellow, or other colors. Sometimes, as in the airplane, they appear to waltz along, then slowly and quietly disappear. Other times they disappear with an explosion.

No one knows how a lightning ball gets inside houses. All that remains when the lightning disappears is the horrible smell of sulphur—and, of course, the damage to property. But there is nothing to fear in a lightning ball. Unlike lightning itself, balls of lightning rarely hurt anyone.

A Good Storm Can Give You a "Lift"

Sometimes storms can play frightening tricks on people. In Sherman, Texas, a farmer was milking his cow in a shed. A storm could be seen in the distance. After a few minutes the storm moved in. The farmer, his cow, and the shed were lifted a few feet off the ground. The man wasn't touched. In fact, not a drop of milk was spilled from his pail! But this is not the only strange storm story.

In a St. Louis tornado, a carpet was lifted from a floor, tacks and all, just as if a skillful upholsterer had used his hammer. The rug was later found hundreds of feet from the house but undamaged. A man was taken by a tornado from his bed, mattress and all, and deposited in a vacant lot. His fall must have been cushioned by the mattress because he wasn't hurt.

A tornado blast ripped the roof off one house and carried away a child. Amazingly, the child landed safely in front of a house six blocks away!

No one really knows what causes tornadoes or why they behave as they do. Photos of tornadoes sometimes show columns of light glowing near their funnels. Perhaps this means that tornadoes give off electricity. The burning effects of some tornadoes and the radio energy that seems to surround them are also mysterious. No one is quite sure if electricity is really produced by the tornado or if it causes the tornado in the first place.

Watch Out for Objects from the Sky

In 1833 many people in New Jersey and New York observed a famous meteor flash through the sky. They also saw "fiery rain." On the ground after that display by nature, strange lumps of jelly-like substances were found. Each lump was like soft soap, about the size of a man's fist.

The lumpy masses were given a name—*star jelly*. Many strange examples of star jelly have been found throughout the world. According to legend and poetry, star jelly is always related to meteors or falling stars. Since it it is so soft, no one knows how it could possibly survive the fiery fall from the sky onto the earth.

In Sweden a very strange collection of jelly-like globes were sighted against the sun's glow. Each was about the size of a volley ball—except *these* volley balls had tails. Large numbers of these balls appeared to block some of the sunlight. The balls floated down to earth, then finally disappeared like soap bubbles. No one can explain what the jelly-like material was.

Between 1756 and 1763 Austria was at war with Prussia. About three o'clock one afternoon, during a lull in battle, some Austrian soldiers felt they were still being attacked. It was raining, but something other than rain was also pounding down on the troops—objects about the size of hazelnuts. When they took off their three-cornered hats and looked in the folded brims, the soldiers were speechless. Their hats were filled with dozens of tiny toads.

One man held up his handkerchief and, sure enough, it was soon filled with tiny toads. The

For centuries soldiers have faced the dangers of war, but when the enemy is joined by the mysterious forces of nature, there are more than bullets to duck.

little animals had tails and seemed to be in the tadpole stage.

There are many examples of these "living rainfalls" throughout history. Toads, frogs, even fish have appeared to drop from the sky. Four such "falls" have occurred recently in the United States.

Of course, a mischievous tornado might be responsible for these mysterious "animal storms." The tornado could have lifted an entire pond and carried it several miles. But why do these falls consist of only one selected species, not the entire population of the pond? More mysterious—why are all the animals the same size? Next time someone says, "It's raining cats and dogs," he may not be kidding!

**And Speaking
of Weather . . .**

. . . lightning flashes, from cloud to earth, can be as long as 20 miles! Giant lightning bolts can get *hot*—about 30,000°C—over five times hotter than the sun's surface!

. . . hailstones bigger than snowballs came down on the town of Coffeyville, Kansas in September, 1970. The hailstones were measured at 17½ inches around and weighed over a pound and one-half each!

. . . when your friends complain about the rainy weather, tell them about Mt. Waialeale in Kauai, Hawaii, where it rains about 350 days each year!

. . . and for those who complain when it's been cloudy for a day or two, a good place to think about is the North Pole. During the North Pole winter—that's a 186 day season—*there is no sun at all!*

The Mirage: Fata Morgana

There are many legends of the sea. They have been told by sailors who roamed the seas over thousands of years. Most are simply tales that everyone knows are not true, but they are fun to tell and hear. Sometimes, however, there is a legend that is surrounded by such mystery and unexplained facts that people wonder if there just might be some truth behind it.

One such legend is the story of Morgan le Fay, the fairy sister of the famous King Arthur. A beautiful woman, she lured sailors from their ships when they passed near her home. Le Fay was said to live in a great castle under the sea near the Strait of Messina.

In 1773, near Reggio, Italy, not far from Messina, a Dominican friar, Antonio Minasi,

A 1903 drawing of Queen Morgan le Fay.

was watching the sunrise over the sea. When the rays had reached a certain angle on the water, he saw an amazing sight. "Arches, castles, columns, towers, palaces with balconies, alleys of trees, plains with herds and flocks, armies of men on foot and horseback"—he said, "and they all seemed to float on the water." Was it a *mirage* the friar was seeing? (A mirage is an illusion, caused by reflections of distant objects over water, desert sands, or hot pavement.)

The friar looked again and saw the same sight reflected in the air above. Then all the objects seemed to flash in beautiful red, green, and blue colors.

This sight has become famous. It is the mirage called *Fata Morgana*, named after the beautiful fairy. It is now known that the castles are a reflection of the coast of Sicily and other parts of Italy even farther away. But no one knows exactly how the magical water and air mirrors work.

A type of mirage—the Fata Morgana—is named for Queen Morgan le Fay. The largest of these was seen in 1913, in the arctic. It was a distant reflection of hills, snow covered peaks, and valleys called "Crocker Land" discovered in 1907 by Admiral Peary.

Many other well-known mirages have been reported. One was sighted off the coast of Cornwall, England in 1914. This mirage had legendary sunken castles, bears, whales, and dancers. It also had a mysterious double image of a ship with a blue funnel. On one side of the horizon, a captain saw a ship with its funnel enlarged. On the other he saw the exact same ship with a normal-sized funnel. No one could explain—was it one ship or two?

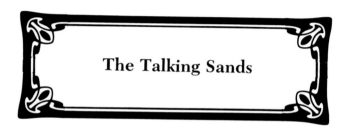

The Talking Sands

The steep slopes of a tall mountain called Jebel Nagous in the Sinai Desert of Egypt are covered with desert sand. The sand is very finely ground and made up of quartz and sandstone grains. When the sand slides, musical tones can be heard. They sound like the base notes of an organ.

The native *Bedouins* (Arabic desert people) believe the sound is a wooden gong from a monastery buried in the mountain. They only hear its music at prayer time.

In the eastern part of Churchill County, Nevada, there is a sandy hill four miles long and one mile wide. None of its sand particles are larger than a pinhead. The sand is so tightly packed that a scurrying lizard, instead of sinking in, causes the sand to slide. The vibrations sound like the singing of telegraph wires and can be heard for six or seven miles. But if a person is too close, the sound of the shifting sand can be *deafening*.

Chapter

4

PUZZLING
PEOPLE

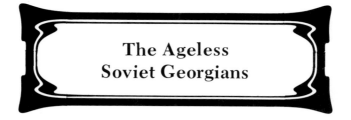

The Ageless
Soviet Georgians

In the Caucasus Mountains of Russia, a land known for its beautiful climate, live the world's healthiest—and oldest—people. These are the citizens of Soviet Georgia. There are over nine million Soviet Georgians. That's as many inhabitants as there are in New York City. *In 1970 at least 5,000 of them were over 100 years old!*

Probably the oldest Soviet Georgian was Shirali Mislomov, called Baba or baby, for

With no way of checking, many scientists feel that Soviet Georgian ages are exaggerated. The oldest human whose birth records were checked was a New York woman—Mrs. Delina Filkins who was born in 1815 and died in 1928, more than 113 years later.

short. He died at 168 years of age, the eldest member of five living generations of Mislomovs. He even had one *great, great, great* grandchild. Mislomov left behind a wife who was 120 years old. *The Mislomovs had been married for 102 years.*

Many of the people look much younger than they are. How do they do it? It is said that their diet consists of fruits, vegetables, cheese, and yoghurt. The climate is favorable and their work habits are moderate. One Georgian told a western news reporter, "I never had a single enemy. I read no books and have no worries." The reporter says he wondered about that answer afterwards—"*Maybe it's really better to read a little, worry a little, and live a shorter life.*"

42

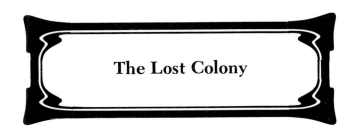

The Lost Colony

Roanoke Island, North Carolina was discovered and settled by the English in 1584. The first winter was difficult for the colonists, but they survived. After a few years, Governor John White decided to sail for England to get more supplies and to bring over more settlers.

He left behind his wife, daughter, and grandchild. His granddaughter, Virginia Dare, was the first European child born in the New World.

But because England was fighting a war with Spain, White was delayed. Three years later, he was finally able to return to North Carolina. As his ship approached the island, the colony seemed deserted. White heard no shouts of welcome. In fact, he heard no sounds at all.

All the people had vanished. Only the homes and fort remained. They were undamaged. They seemed to be in the same condition as when he left them three years earlier. But where were the 121 colonists? Where were his wife and family? White checked for any sign of battle. But there was none. There weren't even signs of a speedy retreat. White was grief-stricken.

White found the word "Croatan" scratched on the bark of a tree near the fort. Nearby he found another tree with the letters "CRO." But White never found out what happened to the lost colony. Perhaps they left Roanoke and sailed for the nearby Croatan Island. Maybe they were shipwrecked on the way. Or perhaps they were killed by the Spanish.

One hundred years later, white hunters visited Robeson County, North Carolina, for the first time. They found a tribe of unusual Indians. They all had blue eyes! The 1790 census revealed that 54 of the 95 Indian names matched those of the lost colony. Were they descendants of the Roanoke settlers?

Today the tribe still exists. Its members speak English. In fact, they use phrases no one has heard since the time of Shakespeare.

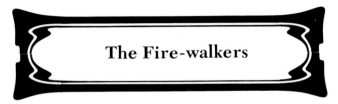

The Fire-walkers

On the island of Tahiti, there are people who can walk slowly through a wide pit filled with red-hot coals—really volcanic rocks. No one has been able to find a blister on any part of their feet. These fire-walkers believe they are priests, and if they have faith, they will somehow be protected.

Some people claim that the rocks aren't really that hot. They also say the fire-walkers know the coolest paths to walk. But one of the people watching the "fire-walk" tried to get close enough to throw his handkerchief on the hot

rocks. The heat kept him from getting close to the pit. One of the fire-walkers took the handkerchief and dropped it on the coals. The cloth immediately turned to ashes.

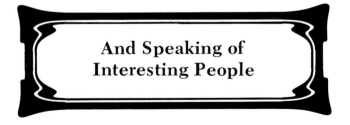

And Speaking of Interesting People

. . . the hottest known fire-walk was by a Mr. Vernon E. Craig, who calls himself "Komar." In

March, 1975, "Komar" walked almost 25 feet on a 1,183°F. surface!

. . . many sword-swallowers really do "swallow" the metal blade. The longest sword "swallowed" was 27 inches by a Mr. Linton of Ireland. (He later "swallowed" four such swords at once.) A Floridian woman, Sandra Reed, has "swallowed" five blades at once—each blade measuring 20 inches in length!

. . . the people of Yap, an island near the Philippines, in the southwestern Pacific Ocean, have an interesting money system. Their coins are probably the largest in the world—*often standing 12 feet high and weighing more than a ton*! The Yap coin is a ground stone with a hole bored through the center. A man can roll his money from place to place by running a wood axle through the hole!

. . . Yap families display their coins outside their houses. Money is never given or taken when something is sold. Instead, things bought or sold are described as trades written on the face of the coin. The family that is owed something writes it on their own coin and records the debt on the coin of the family who must pay them!

The island of Yap is still one place where money goes a long way!

There are other mysteries of life. Some are very old. Others are being born even as you are reading. You may find them difficult to believe. Everyone finds them hard to explain. But they are true. They are simply unsolved, as yet. Who knows, maybe it will be *you* who will someday solve one of the many strange mysteries of life.